# THE OUTLINE WIZARD

**WRITTEN BY LOIS F. ROETS**
**ILLUSTRATED BY BEV ARMSTRONG**

W9-COB-108

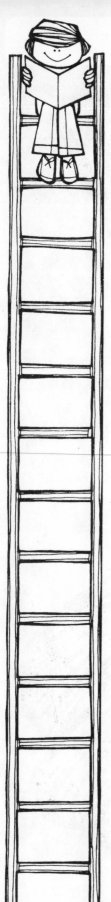

# THE LEARNING WORKS
## P.O. Box 6187 Santa Barbara, CA 93160

The purchase of this book entitles the
individual teacher to reproduce copies for use
in the classroom.

The reproduction of any part for an entire
school or school system or for commercial
use is strictly prohibited.

No form of this work may be reproduced
or transmitted or recorded without written
permission from the publisher.

Copyright © 1980 — THE LEARNING WORKS, INC.
All rights reserved.
Printed in the United States of America.

Name _____

An *outline* is a summary arrangement of information that explains and describes a given topic. *Outlining* saves time and makes learning easier.

Each outline should have a *title*. The title tells what the outline is about.

Sample Title: Kinds of Food

The *main topic* is a word or short phrase that is related to the outline title. The main topics are marked with Roman numerals: I, II, III, IV, or as many as are needed.

Sample outline with title and main entries:

| | |
|---|---|
| *(Topic)* | Kinds of Food |
| *(Main topic)* | I. Vegetables |
| *(Main topic)* | II. Fruits |
| *(Main topic)* | III. Meats |

## REVIEW

1. What is an outline? _____

_____

2. What does the title of an outline tell? _____

_____

3. What is the title for the sample outline listed above? _____

_____

4. What do main topics tell about? _____

_____

5. What are the three main topics in the sample outline?

    I. _____

    II. _____

    III. _____

Name _____

---

Each of the main entries (I, II, III, etc.) can be explained more fully. The entries that explain a main topic are *subentries*. A *subentry* explains the main entry. To show that a *subentry* is giving information about the main entry, the subentry is indented (moved in) and placed under the main entry that it is explaining. These subentries are labeled with letters; A, B, C, or as many as needed.

---

Sample outline with title, main topics and subentries:

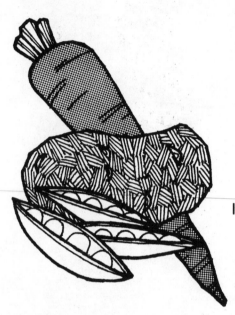

Kinds of Food

I. Vegetables
   A. Carrots
   B. Peas
   C. Potatoes

II. Fruits
   A. Grapes
   B. Peaches
   C. Apples

III. Meats
   A. Pork
   B. Beef
   C. Poultry

## REVIEW

1. What is the title of this outline? _____

2. This outline has three *main topics* that explain the title. What are the three *main topics*?

    I. _____

    II. _____

    III. _____

3. In this outline, each of the three main entries has *subentries* that describe the main entries. List the subentries for "Vegetables."

_____  _____  _____

4. List the subentries for "Fruits."

_____  _____  _____

5. List the subentries for "Meats."

_____  _____  _____

COPYRIGHT © 1980 — THE LEARNING WORKS, INC.

Name _____

Each outline *subentry* can be described more fully. To give more information about a *subentry*, indent (move in) and list the information. This information is numbered as 1, 2, 3, or as many numbers as are needed.

Note: A single entry is not allowed when a *subentry* is used. It must be accompanied by at least one other *subentry*.

Improper Outline — Single subentry
   I.  Vegetables
      A. Carrots
  II.  Fruits

Proper Outline
   I.  Vegetables
      A. Carrots
      B. Peas
  II.  Fruits

Sample outline with title, main topics and two kinds of subentries:

Kinds of Food

   I.  Vegetables
      A. Grapes
      B. Peas
      C. Potatoes

  II.  Fruits
      A. Grapes
      B. Peaches
      C. Apples
         1. Golden Delicious
         2. Red Delicious

 III.  Meats
      A. Pork
      B. Beef
      C. Poultry
         1. Chicken
         2. Turkey
         3. Duck

# REVIEW

1. Golden Delicious and Red Delicious describe which subentry? _____

2. Chicken, turkey and duck describe which subentry? _____

COPYRIGHT © 1980 — THE LEARNING WORKS, INC.

Name _____

Read the paragraphs. Transfer the underlined information to the outline below the paragraphs. The type of line is a hint as to where the information should be placed.

## ANIMALS WITH FUR

There are many animals with fur. Some common furry animals are the cat, dog and rabbit. These animals we often see.

Other furry animals are not seen so often. Uncommon furry animals might be a lion, fox and bear. The Arctic fox and the red fox are two kinds of furry foxes. A grizzly bear, a brown bear and a polar bear are three kinds of furry bears.

I. _____

   A. _____

      1. _____

      2. _____

      3. _____

   B. _____

      1. _____

      2. _____

         a. _____

         b. _____

      3. _____

         a. _____

         b. _____

         c. _____

COPYRIGHT © 1980 — THE LEARNING WORKS, INC.

Name _____

Read the paragraphs. Transfer the underlined information to the outline below the paragraphs. The type of line is a hint as to where the information should be placed in the outline.

## FAST AND SLOW MOVING ANIMALS

Many animals can move at high rates of speed. The cheetah can run 60-63 miles per hour (m.p.h.) over level ground. He cannot run long distances at that speed. The pronghorn antelope can run long distances at high speed. The pronghorn antelope can run 35 m.p.h. for 4 miles, 42 m.p.h. for 1 mile and 55 m.p.h. for ½ mile. You could not outrun the cheetah or pronghorn antelope.

Some animals move very slowly. The slowest moving land mammal is the three-toed sloth, which moves at only .068 m.p.h. The common garden snail moves at .03 miles per hour. The giant tortoise moves at the rate of .17 miles per hour.

## FAST AND SLOW MOVING ANIMALS

I. _____

  A. _____

    _____

  B. _____

    _____

      1. _____

      2. _____

      3. _____

II. _____

  A. _____

    _____

  B. _____

    _____

  C. _____

    _____

COPYRIGHT © 1980 — THE LEARNING WORKS, INC.     

Name _____

Read the paragraphs. Transfer the underlined information to the outline below the paragraphs. The type of line is a hint as to where the information should be placed.

# PRODUCTS MADE FROM SOMETHING ELSE

Today we hear much about oil. <u>Many products are made from oil.</u> Some products made from oil are plastic, ink, paint and medicine.

Wood is also useful. <u>Many products come from wood.</u> Some products that come from wood are lumber, toothpicks and paper.

Grains grow in fields. <u>Many products come from grain.</u> Some products from grain are vegetable oil, bread and breakfast cereals, such as Corn Flakes and Puffed Wheat.

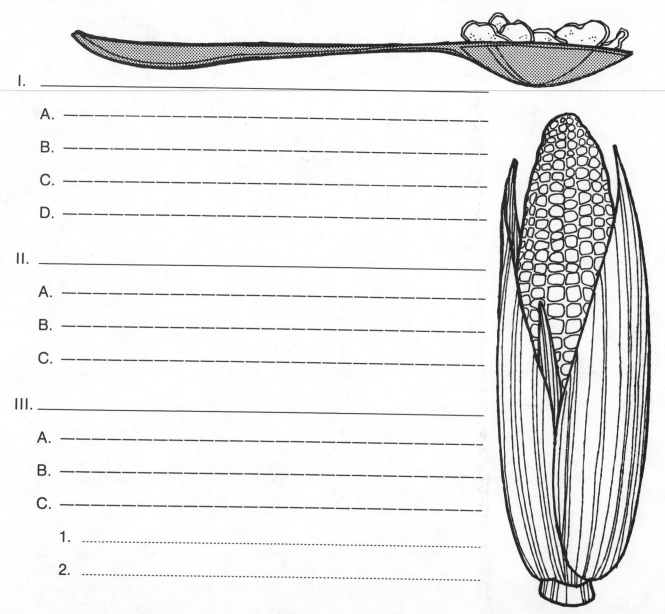

I. _____

   A. _____

   B. _____

   C. _____

   D. _____

II. _____

   A. _____

   B. _____

   C. _____

III. _____

   A. _____

   B. _____

   C. _____

      1. _____

      2. _____

COPYRIGHT © 1980 — THE LEARNING WORKS, INC.

Name _____

## PLANNING A PARTY

Mary and Janice were planning a party for their friends.

"Let's serve delicious chocolate cake," said Mary. "To make the cake, I'll need a box of chocolate cake mix, a few eggs, vegetable oil and water. For the frosting I'll buy two boxes of frosting mix so the frosting can be extra thick. All I need to add to the boxes of frosting mix are water and margarine."

"That sounds good but I was thinking about making pizza," said Janice. "We wouldn't need knives and forks — only lots of napkins! If we serve pizza, we would need pizza dough, tomato paste, cheese, oregano, garlic, salt and pepper."

"That's a good idea, too," said Mary. "Let's think about it for awhile. The party isn't for another week. We can decide later."

Which would you prefer?

Read the story above. Complete the outline with information from the story.

I. Things the girls will need to serve chocolate cake:

   A. Box of chocolate cake mix and three ingredients:

      1. _____

      2. _____

      3. _____

   B. Boxes of frosting mix and two ingredients:

      1. _____

      2. _____

II. Things the girls will need to make pizza:

   A. _____

   B. _____

   C. _____

   D. Spices

      1. _____

      2. _____

      3. _____

      4. _____

Name _____

Complete this outline. **Remember:** The **first** word of each outline entry begins with a capital letter.

## MY FAVORITE THINGS

I.  My favorite games

    A. _____

    B. _____

    C. _____

    D. _____

II. People I like to be with

    A. _____

    B. _____

    C. _____

    D. _____

III. My favorite sandwiches

    A. _____

    B. _____

    C. _____

IV. My favorite books

    A. _____

    B. _____

    C. _____

V.  Some of my hobbies and special interests

    A. _____

    B. _____

    C. _____

COPYRIGHT © 1980 — THE LEARNING WORKS, INC.

Name _____

Complete this outline. Each word must be spelled correctly. **Remember:** The **first** word of each outline entry begins with a capital letter.

## PRACTICAL GIFTS TO GIVE AND RECEIVE

I. Gifts that can be worn as clothing

    A. _____

    B. _____

    C. _____

    D. _____

    E. _____

    F. _____

    G. _____

II. Gifts that can help someone fix broken furniture or make home repairs

    A. _____

    B. _____

    C. _____

    D. _____

III. Gifts that give us something fun to do

    A. _____

    B. _____

    C. _____

    D. _____

    E. _____

COPYRIGHT © 1980 — THE LEARNING WORKS, INC.

Name _____

Complete this outline by filling in subentries that describe the main entry. **Remember:**
Each entry begins with a capital letter. Try to spell each word correctly.

## LISTING ITEMS

I.  Things found at a picnic

   A. _____

   B. _____

   C. _____

   D. _____

   E. _____

II. Things seen at a football game

   A. _____

   B. _____

   C. _____

   D. _____

III. Things found in the kitchen

   A. _____

   B. _____

   C. _____

   D. _____

   E. _____

   F. _____

IV. Things found in a pet shop

   A. _____

   B. _____

   C. _____

Name _____

Complete this outline with information you know or can find. You might want to look in the sports section of the newspaper, in an encyclopedia, or ask a friend for some ideas. **Remember:** Each entry in an outline begins with a capital letter.

## SPORTING EVENTS

I.  Sporting events in which two people play against each other

   A. _____

   B. _____

   C. _____

   D. _____

II. Sporting events played by a pair — two players compete with two opposing players

   A. _____

   B. _____

   C. _____

III. Sporting events played by a team — three or more players compete with a team of three or more players

   A. _____

   B. _____

   C. _____

   D. _____

   E. _____

   F. _____

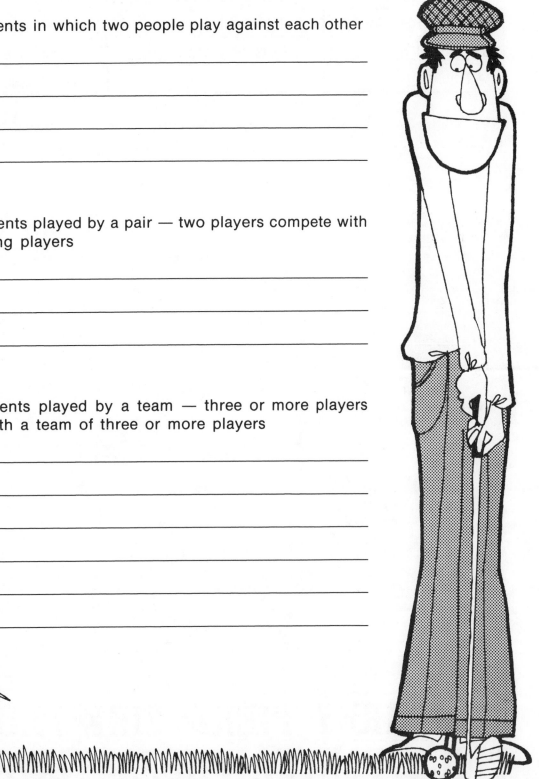

Name _____

Read all the outline entries listed in the box. Arrange all entries into their proper sequence. You may cut apart the entries as a help to arranging them. Write the entries into the outline given.

| Comics | Cover | Glossary |
|---|---|---|
| Headlines | Names of cities | Names of mountains |
| Names of rivers | Names of states | News articles |
| Parts of a book | Parts of a U.S. map | Parts of a newspaper |
| Title page | Scale of miles | Want ads |

I. _____

  A. _____

  B. _____

  C. _____

II. _____

  A. _____

  B. _____

  C. _____

  D. _____

III. _____

  A. _____

  B. _____

  C. _____

  D. _____

  E. _____

# PUMPHREY PIERZ PIKE PECULIAR
# PIQUA PLEVNA PHEBA PECATONICA

COPYRIGHT © 1980 — THE LEARNING WORKS, INC.

Name _____

Read and study this outline.  Use the outline to answer the questions.

## TURTLES

I. Turtles are reptiles with shells.
  A. Turtles are cold-blooded animals who cannot live in the Arctic.
  B. Names commonly used are: turtle, tortoise and terrapin.
  C. Turtles are the only group of higher animals that have most of their bony parts on the outside.

II. Not all turtles live the same kind of life.
  A. There are land turtles.
    1. Land turtles are slow and clumsy.
    2. The bones of their shells are closely joined to give protection.
  B. There are fresh-water turtles.
    1. Fresh-water turtles are active and can move quickly.
    2. Their toes are webbed.
  C. There are sea turtles.
    1. Sea turtles have paddle-shaped legs.
    2. Their shell bones are loosely joined and are quite flat.

III. There are some interesting facts about the turtle.
  A. Turtles have been around for 175,000,000 years.
  B. Turtles have no teeth.
    1. They have jaws with horny edges for biting.
    2. Turtles eat animals, plants and decayed flesh.
  C. The leatherneck turtle (a sea turtle) can weigh 3/4 of a ton.
  D. Dark red turtle meat tastes like beef.

1. What is the title of this outline? _____

2. What three kinds of turtles are talked about in this outline?

_____   _____   _____

3. Of the fresh-water or land turtles, which kind usually moves more quickly?

_____

4. What do turtles eat? _____, _____, _____

5. You may call it a turtle. What are two other names used to describe these reptiles

  with bony shells? _____ and _____

6. Could you make a necklace of turtle's teeth?  Explain your answer.

_____

7. What kind of turtles have paddle-shaped legs? _____

8. How does the shell help the turtle? _____

_____

Name _____

Read and study this outline.  Use the outline to answer the questions.

# PIRATES AND STOLEN TREASURES

I.  Real pirates of long ago
    A. Uruj Barbarossa; 1500s, pirated between parts of Italy and Spain
    B. Khair-ed-Din; 1600s, pirated in Mediterranean Sea
    C. Pirate Jean Lafitte; early 1800s, pirated in Gulf of Mexico
    D. Captain Kidd; 1600s, pirated waters of the Atlantic Ocean
    E. Blackbeard
        1. Braided his long black beard
        2. Pirated around Carolina and Virginia, 1716-1718

II. Other words used to describe a pirate
    A. Buccaneer
    B. Corsair
    C. Freebooter

III. Valuable items pirates often stole
    A. Gems
    B. Food and supplies
    C. Money

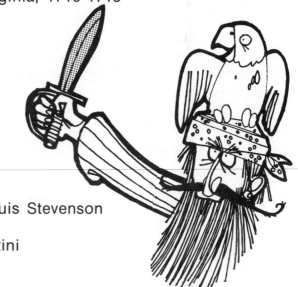

IV. Fiction books about pirates
    A. TREASURE ISLAND, by Robert Louis Stevenson
    B. PETER PAN, by Sir James Barrie
    C. CAPTAIN BLOOD, by Rafael Sabatini

1. List three things often stolen by pirates. _____ ,
_____ and _____

2. How did the pirate Blackbeard get his name? _____
_____

3. List four names for people who steal things from other people's ships:
_____

4. If you wanted to read a book about a pirate, what are three books you could read?
    a. _____
    b. _____
    c. _____

5. One pirate helped our country defend New Orleans in the War of 1812. Which pirate do you think this was?  (Hint: Read dates and locations for each pirate.)
_____

Outside reference:  For additional information, look in the encyclopedia and read about some of the following pirates: Sir Francis Drake, Captain Kidd, Blackbeard.

Name _____

Read and study this outline.  Use the outline to answer the questions.

## USEFUL INVENTIONS

I.  Inventions that helped home and family life
   A. Canned foods: Nicolas Appert, France, 1787-1810
   B. Safety match: Gustave E. Pasch, Sweden, 1844
   C. Safety pin: Walter Hunt, United States, 1846
   D. Sewing machine: Elias Howe, United States, 1845
   E. Lawn mower: Edwin Budding, Great Britain, 1830
   F. Carpet sweeper: Melville R. Bissell, United States, 1876

II. Inventions that helped science and industry
   A. Telescope: Hans Lippershey, Netherlands, 1608
   B. Adding machine: Blaise Pascal, France, 1642
   C. Elevator: Elisha G. Otis, United States, 1853

III. Inventions that helped agriculture
   A. Cotton gin: Eli Whitney, United States, 1793
   B. Reaper: Cyrus H. McCormick, United States, 1834
   C. Barbed wire: Joseph Glidden, United States, 1873
   D. Tractor: Benjamin Holt, United States, 1904

1. List four inventions that helped farmers. _____ ,
_____ , _____ and _____ .

2. We can preserve foods in cans for long periods of time. We can be thankful to
_____ for this invention.

3. In this outline, eight inventions and inventors are from the United States. List
them and their inventions.

| INVENTORS | INVENTIONS |
|---|---|
| a. _____ | _____ |
| b. _____ | _____ |
| c. _____ | _____ |
| d. _____ | _____ |
| e. _____ | _____ |
| f. _____ | _____ |
| g. _____ | _____ |
| h. _____ | _____ |

4. If you lose a button, which invention listed might you use?
_____ . Who invented it? _____

5. What is the earliest invention listed in this outline? _____
Invented by _____ in the year _____ .

COPYRIGHT © 1980 — THE LEARNING WORKS, INC.

Name _____

Read and study this outline.  Use the outline to answer the questions.

# CATS

I.  Description of a cat
   A.  All cats have coats of fine, shiny hair.
   B.  Cat's teeth
      1.  Kittens have 26 needle-like teeth called milk teeth.
      2.  Adult cats have 30 teeth.
   C.  Cats have two sets of vocal cords.
      1.  One set of vocal cords is used to "meow."
      2.  One set of vocal cords is used to purr and to growl.
   D.  Cat's eyes
      1.  In daytime, the iris of a cat's eye narrows to shut out glare from light.
      2.  At nighttime, the iris of the eye widens to let in light.
   E.  Cat's paws
      1.  Cats have five toes on each forefoot and four toes on each hindfoot.
      2.  Cats shed their claws at various times throughout the year.

II.  Kinds of cats
   A.  Short-haired cats include: Domestic Shorthair, Siamese, Abyssinian, Russian Blue, Manx and Rex.
   B.  Long-haired cats include: Angora, Persian and Himalayan.

III.  Common expressions that refer to cats
   A.  "Curiosity killed a cat" — somebody who always looks into other people's business may get into trouble.
   B.  "When the cat's away, the mice will play" — a person may get into trouble when no one is there to watch him.

1.  What is the title of this outline? _____

2.  What are the two main groups of cats? _____

3.  How many teeth do kittens have? _____

   What is another word for a kitten's teeth? _____

4.  Why does the iris of a cat's eye change during the day and the night?  Explain your answer.

   _____

   _____

5.  Cats have two sets of vocal cords. With these, they can make three sounds. What are these three sounds?

   _____

6.  Explain the expression "When the cat's away, the mice will play."

   _____

   _____

Name _____

Read entries I, II and III. Use the entries listed in the box below the outline to complete the outline. If the entry is a fish, write it under "Fin." If the entry has hair or fur, write it under "Fur." If the entry is a bird, write it under "Feathers." **Remember:** All entries begin with a capital letter.

## FIN, FUR, FEATHERS

I.  Fin

    A. _____

    B. _____

    C. _____

    D. _____

    E _____

II. Fur

    A. _____

    B. _____

    C. _____

    D. _____

    E. _____

III. Feathers

    A. _____

    B. _____

    C. _____

    D. _____

    E. _____

| | | | | |
|---|---|---|---|---|
| Bluegill | Bluejay | Bullhead | Cardinal | Cat |
| Cow | Haddock | Lion | Meadowlark | Monkey |
| Parrot | Perch | Sparrow | Tiger | Trout |

Name _____

Complete entries I, II and III. Use entries listed in the box below. **Remember:** Each
entry begins with a capital letter and must describe the entry under which it is placed.

| | | |
|---|---|---|
| Baking powder | Grass scissors | Pruning clippers |
| Construction paper | Lawn mower | Rake |
| Eggs | Milk | Sugar |
| Flour | Paint | Wooden frame |
| Glue | | |

## WHAT BELONGS TO WHAT?

I. Ingredients of a cake

A. _____

B. _____

C. _____

D. _____

E. _____

II. Equipment for an art project

A. _____

B. _____

C. _____

D. _____

III. Equipment for yard work

A. _____

B. _____

C. _____

D. _____

Name _____

Read entries I and II listed below.  Use the entries listed in the box to complete the outline. **Remember:** Each entry begins with a capital letter and must describe the main entry under which it is placed.

I.  Athletic activities

    A. _____

    B. _____

    C. _____

    D. _____

    E. _____

    F. _____

    G. _____

    H. _____

    I. _____

    J. _____

    K. _____

    L. _____

II.  Board games

    A. _____

    B. _____

    C. _____

    D. _____

    E. _____

    F. _____

Basketball

Football

Monopoly

Baseball

Wrestling

Chess

Chinese checkers

Soccer

Scrabble

Golf

Table tennis

Backgammon

Roller skating

Boxing

Skiing

Dominoes

Polo

Bowling

COPYRIGHT © 1980 — THE LEARNING WORKS, INC.

Name _____

Complete entries I, II, III, IV, V and VI. Use entries listed in the box. **Remember:**
Each entry begins with a capital letter and must describe the entry under which
it is placed.

## SPORTS EQUIPMENT

I. Equipment to play baseball

    A. _____

    B. _____

    C. _____

II. Equipment to play basketball

    A. _____

    B. _____

III. Equipment to play tennis

    A. _____

    B. _____

    C. _____

IV. Equipment for water skiing

    A. _____

    B. _____

    C. _____

V. Equipment for playing hockey

    A. _____

    B. _____

    C. _____

VI. Equipment for playing football

    A. _____

    B. _____

Box:
Baseball
Basketball
Bat
Cage
Football
Glove
Hockey stick
Hoop
Motor boat
Net
Puck
Racquets
Tennis balls
Tow rope
Water skis
Helmet

Name _____

Read entries I, II and III listed below. Use the entries listed in the box to complete the outline. **Remember:** Each entry begins with a capital letter and must describe the main entry under which it is placed.

## THINGS I NEED

I.  Things used in school

   A. _____

   B. Writing instruments

      1. _____

      2. _____

   C. Kinds of paper

      1. _____

      2. _____

      3. _____

II. Things needed to make a vegetable garden

   A. _____

   B. Tools

      1. _____

      2. _____

   C. Seeds

      1. _____

      2. _____

      3. _____

III. Things needed to build a dog house

   A. _____

   B. Tools

      1. _____

      2. _____

   C. Supplies

      1. _____

      2. _____

      3. _____

* * * * * * * * * * * *
* Nails
* Looseleaf paper
* Books
* Carrots
* Pens
* Hammer
* Building plan
* Ground, sunlight, water
* Lettuce
* Spiral notebooks
* Saw
* Shovel
* Pencils
* Construction paper
* Rake
* Radishes
* Boards
* Paint
* * * * * * * * * * * *

Name _____

Read all the outline entries listed in the box. Arrange all the entries into their proper order. You may cut apart the entries and arrange them. Write the entries into the outline.

## FOOD GROUPS

| Outline | | Box |
|---------|---|-----|
| I. _____ | | Apples |
|   A. _____ | | Bananas |
|   B. _____ | | Beef |
| II. _____ | | Beets |
|   A. _____ | | Bread |
|   B. _____ | | Butter |
|   C. _____ | | Carbohydrates |
| III. _____ | | Carrots |
|   A. _____ | | Celery |
|   B. _____ | | Cereal |
|   C. _____ | | Cheese |
|   D. _____ | | Cherries |
| IV. _____ | | Dairy products |
|   A. _____ | | Fruits |
|   B. _____ | | Grapes |
|   C. _____ | | Ice cream |
|   D. _____ | | Lettuce |
|   E. _____ | | Meat |
| V. _____ | | Milk |
|   A. _____ | | Oranges |
|   B. _____ | | Pork |
|   C. _____ | | Potatoes |
|   D. _____ | | Radishes |
|   E. _____ | | Rice |
|   F. _____ | | Vegetables |

COPYRIGHT © 1980 — THE LEARNING WORKS, INC.

24

Name _____

Read all the outline entries listed in the box. Arrange all the entries into their proper sequence. You may cut apart the entries and arrange them. Then write the entries into the outline given.

## LET THERE BE LIGHT

I. Lights found in nature

   A. _____

   B. _____

   C. _____

   D. _____

II. Electric lights

   A. _____

   B. _____

   C. _____

III. Lights from fire

   A. _____

   B. _____

   C. _____

   D. _____

   E. _____

IV. Battery lights

   A. _____

   B. _____

|  |
| --- |
| Bonfire |
| Camera flash |
| Camp fire |
| Candle flame |
| Street lights |
| Torch lights |
| Fireflies |
| Fireplace |
| Flashlight |
| Lamp |
| Moon |
| Northern lights |
| Stove |
| Sun |

Name _____

Read all the outline entries listed in the box. Arrange all entries into their proper sequence. You may cut apart the entries as a help to arranging them. Write the entries into the outline given.

## WAYS

I. _____

   A. _____

   B. _____

   C. _____

   D. _____

   E. _____

   F. _____

II. _____

   A. _____

   B. _____

   C. _____

III. _____

   A. _____

   B. _____

   C. _____

   D. _____

IV. _____

   A. _____

   B. _____

   C. _____

   D. _____

   E. _____

|  |
|---|
| Bicycle |
| Ways to preserve food |
| Bus |
| Car |
| Conversation |
| With a roller |
| Ways to paint a house |
| Canning |
| Letters |
| With a brush |
| Freezing |
| Plane |
| With a spray attachment |
| Drying |
| Refrigeration |
| Sign language |
| Telegraph |
| Telephone |
| Train |
| Walking |
| Ways to communicate with others |
| Ways of traveling |

COPYRIGHT © 1980 — THE LEARNING WORKS, INC.

Name _____

Read all the outline entries listed in the box. Arrange all the entries into their proper sequence. You may cut apart the entries and arrange them. Write the entries into the outline given.

## NATURE'S COLORS

I. _____

   A. _____

   B. _____

II. _____

   A. _____

   B. _____

   C. _____

III. _____

   A. _____

   B. _____

   C. _____

   D. _____

IV. _____

   A. _____

   B. _____

   C. _____

   D. _____

   E. _____

Box entries:

- Sky
- Things nature often colors red
- Stones
- Dirt
- Things nature often colors green
- Cherries
- Things nature often colors blue
- Raccoons
- Things nature often colors brown
- Grass
- Tree leaves
- Water
- Tree trunks
- Moss
- Strawberries
- Deer
- Tomatoes
- Apples

Name _____

Read all the outline entries listed in the box. Arrange all the entries into their proper sequence. You may cut apart the entries and arrange them. Write the entries into the outline given.

## MACHINES ARE MADE OF MANY PARTS

I. _____

   A. _____

   B. _____

   C. _____

   D. _____

   E. _____

II. _____

   A. _____

   B. _____

   C. _____

   D. _____

III. _____

   A. _____

   B. _____

IV. _____

   A. _____

   B. _____

   C. _____

Parts on a typewriter

Windshield wipers

Pedals

Handlebars

Parts on a bicycle

Cutting blade

Headlights

Parts on a car

Keyboard

Two wheels with spokes

Carburetor

Ribbon

Battery

Parts on a lawn mower

Steering wheel

Roller

Handle

Chain

Name _____

Complete this outline by listing titles of books you have read, TV shows you have watched, and movies you have seen.

In titles of books, TV shows and movies, the first, last and every important word begins with a capital letter.

Samples:  Sesame Street
Little House on the Prairie
My Friend Flicka
Jaws

## ENTERTAINMENT AND INFORMATION

I. Television shows

A. _____

B. _____

C. _____

D. _____

II. Books

A. Biography — books about people

1. _____

2. _____

B. Mystery and adventure books

1. _____

2. _____

C. Books that tell about plants, animals or the universe

1. _____

2. _____

III. Movies

A. _____

B. _____

C. _____

Complete this outline by writing titles.

# WHERE TO FIND INFORMATION

I. Names of newspapers

   A. _____

   B. _____

II. Names of reference books

   A. Encyclopedias

      1. _____

      2. _____

   B. Dictionaries

      1. _____

      2. _____

III. Names of magazines

   A. _____

   B. _____

   C. _____

   D. _____

   E. _____

COPYRIGHT © 1980 — THE LEARNING WORKS, INC.

Using outside or personal information
to complete an outline

Name _____

Use newspapers to complete the outline. **Remember:** Each outline entry begins
with a capital letter.

## TODAY'S NEWS

I.  Titles of articles in the newspaper

    A. _____

    B. _____

    C. _____

    D. _____

    E. _____

II. Well-known people who have their names in the newspaper

    A. _____

    B. _____

    C. _____

    D. _____

    E. _____

III. Titles of comic strips in the newspaper

    A. _____

    B. _____

    C. _____

    D. _____

    E. _____

IV. Things for sale that are listed in the want ads

    A. _____

    B. _____

    C. _____

**BEAGLE PUPPIES FOR SALE -
BOUNCY AND LOVABLE
667- 9855**

COPYRIGHT © 1980 — THE LEARNING WORKS, INC.

Name _____

Use the Yellow Pages of the phone book to complete this outline.

## REPAIRS NEEDED

I. Repair shops that could fix a bicycle

   A. (Shop name) _____

      1. (Shop address) _____

      2. (Shop phone) _____

   B. (Shop name) _____

      1. (Shop address) _____

      2. (Shop phone) _____

II. Repair shops that can fix a car

   A. (Shop name) _____

      1. (Shop address) _____

      2. (Shop phone) _____

   B. (Shop name) _____

      1. (Shop address) _____

      2. (Shop phone) _____

III. Shops that could fix a leaking faucet

   A. (Shop name) _____

      1. (Shop address) _____

      2. (Shop phone) _____

   B. (Shop name) _____

      1. (Shop address) _____

      2. (Shop phone) _____

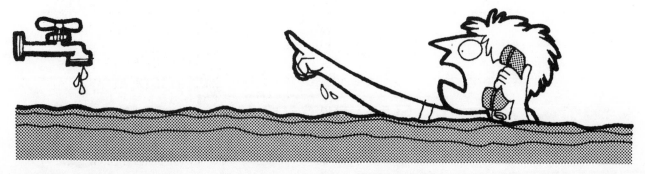

Name _____

Use the Yellow Pages of the phone book to complete this outline.

# USING YELLOW PAGES OF PHONE BOOK

I. Names, addresses and phone numbers of grocery stores

   B. (Store name) _____

      1. (Address) _____

      2. (Phone number) _____

   B. (Store name) _____

      1. (Address) _____

      2. (Phone number) _____

   C. (Store name) _____

      1. (Address) _____

      2. (Phone number) _____

II. Names, addresses and phone numbers of stores that sell paint and paint supplies

   A. (Store name) _____

      1. (Address) _____

      2. (Phone number) _____

   B. (Store name) _____

      1. (Address) _____

      2. (Phone number) _____

III. Names, addresses and phone numbers of barber shops

   A. (Name of office or service) _____

      1. (Address) _____

      2. (Phone) _____

   B. (Name of office or service) _____

      1. (Address) _____

      2. (Phone) _____

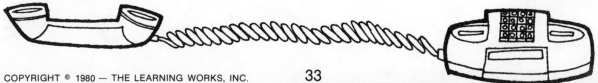

COPYRIGHT © 1980 — THE LEARNING WORKS, INC.

Name _____

Write one paragraph for each short outline listed. Write the paragraph first on scrap paper. After you have corrected it, write the paragraph on the lines below each short outline.

---

Sample:                    I'M GROWING OLDER
                I. Things I played when I was younger
                II. Things I play with now

   I am not the same as when I was young.  I used to play with fingerpaints and blocks.  Now my little sister plays with them.  I like to play baseball and Monopoly.

---

### COST OF THINGS
I. Things I can buy for **less** than one dollar.
II. Things that would cost **more** than one dollar.

_____

_____

_____

_____

### THINKING ABOUT THINGS I HAVE DONE
I. Things I have done but never want to do again
II. Things I have done that I'd like to do again

_____

_____

_____

_____

COPYRIGHT © 1980 — THE LEARNING WORKS, INC.

Name _____

Write one paragraph for each short outline listed. Write the paragraph first on scrap paper. After you have corrected it, write the paragraph on the lines below each short outline. Be sure to use complete sentences.

Sample:          GIFTS I LIKE TO RECEIVE
                I. Clothes to wear
               II. Games to play with my friends

   I like to receive gifts. I like sweaters and shirts in my favorite color, blue. Chess, checkers, and Monopoly are always fun. My friends come and play these games with me.

CHORES I DO AT HOME
I. For others
II. For myself

_____

_____

_____

_____

THE PERFECT VACATION TRIP
I. The place I'd like to go
II. The reason I'd like to go there

_____

_____

_____

_____

_____

COPYRIGHT © 1980 — THE LEARNING WORKS, INC.

Name _____

Write one paragraph for each short outline listed.  Write the paragraph first on scrap paper.  After you have corrected it, write the paragraph on the lines below each short outline.

---

Sample:                          GIFTS I LIKE TO RECEIVE
                          I. Clothes to wear
                          II. Games to play with my friends

   I like to receive gifts. I like books and sweaters in my favorite color, red. Chess, checkers, and dominoes are always appreciated. I enjoy playing these games with my friends.

---

MY FAVORITE HOBBY
I.  What I enjoy doing in my spare time
II.  How I chose this hobby

_____

_____

_____

_____

MY DREAM CAR

I. Design
II. Special features

_____

_____

_____

_____

_____

COPYRIGHT © 1980 — THE LEARNING WORKS, INC.     36

Name _____

Write one paragraph for each short outline listed. Write the paragraph first on scrap paper. After you have corrected the paragraph, write the paragraph on the lines below the short outline.

Sample:          PLANTS AND MORE PLANTS
                     I. House plants
                     II. Garden plants

My neighbor has many house plants. She raises African violets, gloxinias and ferns. I do not have house plants. I have garden plants. I raise these garden plants: lettuce, radishes, carrots and potatoes.

WAYS TO EARN A DOLLAR — OR MORE
   I. Neighborhood jobs
   II. Jobs around the house

_____

_____

_____

_____

_____

MUSIC TO MY EARS
   I. I like to sing to
   II. I like to dance to

_____

_____

_____

COPYRIGHT © 1980 — THE LEARNING WORKS, INC.          37

Name _____

Write one paragraph for each short outline listed. Write the paragraph first on scrap paper. After you have corrected the paragraph, write the paragraph on the lines below the short outline.

---

Sample:                    DOING THINGS WELL
      I. Things I can do well
     II. Things I wish I could do well

   My friends tell me that I draw well. I like the things I draw. I can also dance really well. When I roller skate I fall down a lot. I wish I could skate better. I also would like to sing better.

---

### DREAM A DREAM?
I. Dreams I'd like to have come true
II. Dreams that I hope never come true

_____

_____

_____

_____

_____

### SOUNDS AROUND ME
I. Sounds I might hear on a busy street
II. Sounds I might hear near the river or ocean shore

_____

_____

_____

_____

_____

Name _____

Here is only a part of an outline.  Write a paragraph using the information given.
The first is a sample paragraph based on a part of the outline.

Sample:

A. Favorite subjects I study in school
   1. Reading
   2. Spelling
   3. Music
B. Subjects I study in school that are
   not my favorites
   1. Mathematics
   2. Geography

   Most of the time I like school. I like school when I can study reading,
spelling and music. School isn't the greatest when I must do mathematics
or geography.

I.  Fruits not known to our forefathers
    A. Grapefruit
    B. Banana
    C. Avocado
II. Vegetables not known to our forefathers
    A. Broccoli
    B. Artichoke
    C. Soybeans

_____

_____

_____

_____

## ADDITIONAL PRACTICE IN PARAGRAPH WRITING

I. Card games are fun.
   A. Card games I know how to play
   B. Card games I'd like to learn to play

Name _____

Here is only part of an outline. On scrap paper, write a paragraph using the information given. After you have corrected the paragraph, write the paragraph on the lines listed below the outline. Do the same for each outline. Be sure to use complete sentences.

A. Choosing words for posters
   1. Use short, catchy words
   2. Print letters in large size
B. Materials needed to make a poster
   1. Cardboard
   2. Markers
   3. Pictures

HALLOWEEN CARNIVAL

GAMES·RIDES·PRIZES
OCT. 30 · OAK ST. SCHOOL

_____

_____

_____

_____

_____

_____

A. Gathering information on moths and butterflies
   1. Books on moths and butterflies
   2. Books on collecting moths and butterflies
B. Materials needed for collecting moths and butterflies
   1. Nets
   2. Kill jar
   3. Mounting materials

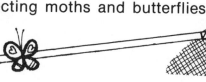

_____

_____

_____

_____

_____

_____

COPYRIGHT © 1980 — THE LEARNING WORKS, INC.

Name _____

Here is only part of an outline. On scrap paper, write a paragraph using the information given. After you have corrected the paragraph, write the paragraph on the
lines listed below the outline. Do the same for each outline. Be sure to use complete
sentences.

A. Sources of energy
   1. Water
   2. Wind
   3. Sun
   4. Fuel
      a. Coal
      b. Natural gas

_____

_____

_____

_____

_____

_____

_____

A. Wise use of natural resources is necessary
   1. Use only what is needed
   2. Learn to conserve energy
B. Each person is responsible for preserving
   his part of the world

_____

_____

_____

_____

_____

_____

_____

Name _____

Study this sample of two paragraphs written from a two-item outline.

---

SUMMER FUN
I. Activities that are fun to do in summer sun
II. Work activities that are done in the summer sun

   In the summer I like to swim, water ski and go hiking.  In the warm summertime I can do many things that are fun.
   There are summer jobs that are done outdoors.  These include lawn cutting and raking, tree trimming and road construction.  Some jobs can only be done in the summertime.

---

Write two paragraphs from the outline below. The information of topic I should be in the first paragraph. The information of topic II should be in the second paragraph. **Note:** Each paragraph should have: (1) an opening sentence, (2) the information from the outline, and (3) a closing sentence. Be sure to use complete sentences.

MONSTERS — MYSTERY OR REAL?

I. Monsters that are real
   A. Hairy Man of Africa was really a gorilla
   B. Sea Serpent was really a giant squid
II. Monsters that may or may not be real
   A. Loch Ness Monster lives in a lake in Scotland
   B. Abominable Snowman is also called the Yeti
   C. Bigfoot lives in the United States

_____

_____

_____

_____

_____

_____

_____

_____

_____

_____

COPYRIGHT © 1980 — THE LEARNING WORKS, INC.

Name _____

Write two paragraphs from this outline.  Write them on scrap paper before writing them on the lines on this paper.  The information of topic I should be in the first paragraph.  The information of topic II should be in the second paragraph.  **Note:** Each paragraph should have: (1) an opening sentence, (2) the information from the outline, and (3) a closing sentence.  Be sure to use complete sentences.

## MYSTERY STORIES

I.  There are necessary parts of a mystery story
    A.  The villain (bad guy) must cause trouble
    B.  A mystery has to be solved
    C.  A hero must solve the mystery
II.  Good style must be part of a good mystery story
    A.  The writer keeps you guessing until the end of the story
    B.  The solution should be a surprise
    C.  The hero has many exciting adventures while solving the mystery

_____

_____

_____

_____

_____

_____

_____

_____

_____

_____

_____

_____

_____

Write three paragraphs from this outline. Write them on scrap paper before writing them on the lines on this paper. The information of topic I should be in the first paragraph. The information of topic II should be in the second paragraph. The information of topic III should be in the third paragraph. **Note:** Each paragraph should have: (1) an opening sentence, (2) the information from the outline, and (3) a closing sentence. Be sure to write complete sentences.

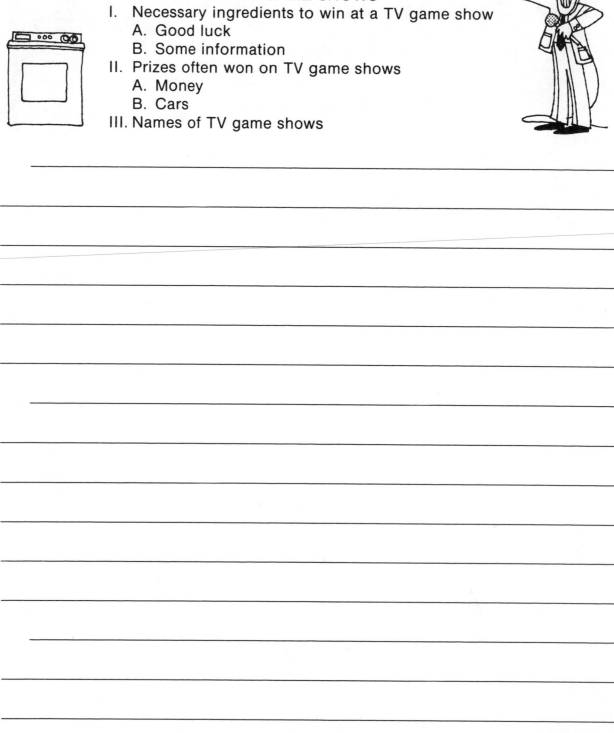

### TV GAME SHOWS

I. Necessary ingredients to win at a TV game show
   A. Good luck
   B. Some information
II. Prizes often won on TV game shows
   A. Money
   B. Cars
III. Names of TV game shows

_____

_____

_____

_____

_____

_____

_____

_____

_____

_____

_____

_____

_____

Name _____

Write three paragraphs from this outline. Write them on scrap paper before writing them on lines on this paper. The information of topic I should be in the first paragraph. The information of topic II should be in the second paragraph. The information of topic III should be in the third paragraph. **Note:** Each paragraph should have: (1) an opening sentence, (2) the information from the outline, and (3) a closing sentence. Be sure to write complete sentences.

## SANDWICHES FOR LUNCH

I. Some cold sandwiches
   A. Necessary ingredients of a cold sandwich
   B. Names of some cold sandwiches
II. Some hot sandwiches
   A. Names of some hot sandwiches
   B. Seasonings often used in hot sandwiches
III. My favorite sandwiches

_____

_____

_____

_____

_____

_____

_____

_____

_____

_____

_____

_____

_____

CERTIFICATE
of WIZARDRY
presented to

_____

on _____

for completing the
OUTLINE WIZARD
awarded by

_____

Copyright © 1980 — THE LEARNING WORKS, INC.

# ANSWERS

**Page 3**
1. An outline is a summary arrangement of information that explains or·describes a given topic.
2. The title tells what the outline is about.
3. Kinds of food
4. Main topics list information related to the outline.
5.   I.   Vegetables
    II.  Fruits
   III.  Meats

**Page 4**
1. Kinds of food
2.   I.   Vegetables
    II.  Fruits
   III.  Meats
3. Carrots, Peas, Potatoes
4. Grapes, Peaches, Apples
5. Pork, Beef, Poultry

**Page 5**
1. Apples
2. Poultry

**Page 6**
I.  Animals with fur
   A.  Common furry animals
      1.  Cat
      2.  Dog
      3.  Rabbit
   B.  Uncommon furry animals
      1.  Lion
      2.  Fox
         a.  Arctic fox
         b.  Red fox
      3.  Bear
         a.  Grizzly bear
         b.  Brown bear
         c.  Polar bear

**Page 7**
I.  Many animals can move at high rates of speed.
   A.  The cheetah can run at 60-63 miles per hour over level ground.
   B.  The pronghorn antelope can run long distances at high speeds.
      1.  35 m.p.h. for 4 miles
      2.  42 m.p.h. for 1 mile
      3.  55 m.p.h. for ½ mile
II.  Some animals move very slowly.
   A.  The slowest moving land animal is the three-toed sloth, which moves at only .068 m.p.h.
   B.  The common garden snail moves at .03 m.p.h.
   C.  The giant tortoise moves at the rate of .17 m.p.h.

**Page 8**
I.  Many products are made from oil.
   A.  Plastic
   B.  Ink
   C.  Paint
   D.  Medicine
II.  Many products come from wood.
   A.  Lumber
   B.  Toothpicks
   C.  Paper
III.  Many products come from grain.
   A.  Vegetable oil
   B.  Bread
   C.  Breakfast cereal
      1.  Corn Flakes
      2.  Puffed Wheat

**Page 9**
I.  A.  1.  A few eggs
        2.  Vegetable oil
        3.  Water
   B.  1.  Water
        2.  Margarine

II.  A.  Pizza dough
   B.  Tomato paste
   C.  Cheese
   D.  Spices
      1.  Oregano
      2.  Garlic
      3.  Salt
      4.  Pepper

**Page 10** — Answers will vary.

**Page 11** — Answers will vary.

**Page 12** — Answers will vary.

**Page 13** — Answers will vary.

**Page 14**
I.  Parts of a book
   A.  Title page
   B.  Cover
   C.  Glossary

II.  Parts of a newspaper
   A.  Comics
   B.  Headlines
   C.  News articles
   D.  Want ads

   III.  Parts of a U.S. map
      A.  Names of rivers
      B.  Names of cities
      C.  Names of states
      D.  Scale of miles
      E.  Names of mountains

**Page 15**
1. Turtles
2. Land turtles, Fresh-water turtles, Sea turtles
3. Fresh-water
4. Animals, plants, decayed flesh
5. Tortoise and terrapin
6. No.  Turtles have no teeth.
7. Sea turtles.
8. Protection

**Page 16**
1. Gems, food and supplies, money
2. Braided his long black beard
3. pirate, buccaneer, corsair and freebooter
4. a. Treasure Island, b. Peter Pan, c. Captain Blood
5. Jean Lafitte

**Page 17**
1. Cotton gin, reaper, barbed wire, and tractor
2. Nicolas Appert
3. 

| INVENTORS | INVENTIONS |
| --- | --- |
| a. Walter Hunt | Safety pin |
| b. Elias Howe | Sewing machine |
| c. Melville Bissell | Carpet sweeper |
| d. Elisha Otis | Elevator |
| e. Eli Whitney | Cotton gin |
| f. Cyrus McCormick | Reaper |
| g. Joseph Glidden | Barbed wire |
| h. Benjamin Holt | Tractor |

4. Safety pin; Walter Hunt
5. Telescope; Hans Lippershey; 1608

**Page 18**
1. Cats
2. Short hair, long hair
3. 26. Milk teeth.
4. Iris widens and narrows to control the amount of light coming into the eye.
5. Purr, meow, growl
6. Answers vary.

**Page 19**
I.  Fin
   A.  Bluegill
   B.  Bullhead
   C.  Haddock
   D.  Perch
   E.  Trout

II.  Fur
   A.  Cat
   B.  Cow
   C.  Lion
   D.  Monkey
   E.  Tiger

   III.  Feathers
      A.  Bluejay
      B.  Cardinal
      C.  Meadowlark
      D.  Parrot
      E.  Sparrow

COPYRIGHT © 1980 — THE LEARNING WORKS, INC.

# Answers — continued

## Page 20
I.   A. Baking powder
    B. Eggs
    C. Flour
    D. Milk
    E. Sugar
II.  A. Construction paper
    B. Glue
    C. Paint
    D. Wooden frame
III. A. Grass scissors
    B. Lawn mower
    C. Pruning clippers
    D. Rake

## Page 21
I.   A. Basketball
    B. Football
    C. Baseball
    D. Wrestling
    E. Soccer
    F. Golf
    G. Table tennis
    H. Roller skating
    I. Boxing
    J. Skiing
    K. Polo
    L. Bowling
II.  A. Monopoly
    B. Chess
    C. Chinese checkers
    D. Scrabble
    E. Backgammon
    F. Dominoes

## Page 22
I.   A. Baseball
    B. Bat
    C. Glove
II.  A. Basketball
    B. Hoop
III. A. Net
    B. Racquets
    C. Tennis balls
IV. A. Motor boat
    B. Tow rope
    C. Water skis
V.  A. Cage
    B. Hockey stick
    C. Puck
VI. A. Football
    B. Helmet

## Page 23
I.   A. Books
    B. Writing instruments
      1. Pens
      2. Pencils
    C. Kinds of paper
      1. Looseleaf paper
      2. Spiral notebooks
      3. Construction paper
II.  A. Ground, sunlight, water
    B. Tools
      1. Hoe
      2. Shovel
    C. Seeds
      1. Lettuce
      2. Carrots
      3. Radishes
III. A. Building plan
    B. Tools
      1. Saw
      2. Hammer
    C. Supplies
      1. Paint
      2. Boards
      3. Nails

## Page 24
I.   Meat
    A. Beef
    B. Pork
II.  Carbohydrates
    A. Bread
    B. Rice
    C. Cereal
III. Dairy products
    A. Butter
    B. Cheese
    C. Ice cream
    D. Milk
IV. Fruits
    A. Apples
    B. Bananas
    C. Cherries
    D. Grapes
    E. Oranges
V.  Vegetables
    A. Beets
    B. Carrots
    C. Celery
    D. Lettuce
    E. Potatoes
    F. Radishes

## Page 25
I.   A. Sun
    B. Northern lights
    C. Moon
    D. Fireflies
II.  A. Street lights
    B. Lamp
    C. Stove
III. A. Bonfire
    B. Camp fire
    C. Candle flame
    D. Torch light
    E. Fireplace
IV. A. Flashlight
    B. Camera flash

## Page 26
I.   Ways of traveling
    A. Bicycle
    B. Bus
    C. Car
    D. Plane
    E. Train
    F. Walking
II.  Ways to paint a house
    A. With a roller
    B. With a brush
    C. With a spray attachment
III. Ways to preserve food
    A. Canning
    B. Freezing
    C. Drying
    D. Refrigeration
IV. Ways to communicate with others
    A. Conversation
    B. Letters
    C. Sign language
    D. Telegraph
    E. Telephone

## Page 27
I.   Things nature often colors blue
    A. Sky
    B. Water
II.  Things nature often colors green
    A. Grass
    B. Tree leaves
    C. Moss
III. Things nature often colors red
    A. Cherries
    B. Strawberries
    C. Tomatoes
    D. Apples
IV. Things nature often colors brown
    A. Stones
    B. Dirt
    C. Raccoons
    D. Tree trunks
    E. Deer

## Page 28
I.   Parts on a car
    A. Windshield wipers
    B. Headlights
    C. Carburetor
    D. Battery
    E. Steering wheel
II.  Parts on a bicycle
    A. Pedals
    B. Handlebars
    C. Two wheels with spokes
    D. Chain
III. Parts on a lawn mower
    A. Cutting blade
    B. Handle
IV. Parts on a typewriter
    A. Keyboard
    B. Ribbon
    C. Roller

**Pages 29-45** — Answers will vary.

COPYRIGHT © 1980 — THE LEARNING WORKS, INC.